The Elves and the Shoemaker

with

The Magic Porridge Pot

Illustrated by Val Biro

Award Publications Limited

Once there was a poor shoemaker. He had only enough leather to make one more pair of shoes.

"I must sew these well. I will start tomorrow," he yawned.

But the next morning, the shoemaker was surprised to find the shoes already finished!

The shoes were perfect and sold straight away! He used the money to buy more leather. He left the cut leather out that night. Next morning, another pair of shoes had appeared. Soon, everyone wanted his wonderful shoes.

The shoemaker was very happy to sell such fine shoes. But who was making them?

One night, he and his wife stayed awake to find out.

To their surprise, two elves appeared and sewed the leather he had cut.

"The elves have helped us so much," said his wife. "We must repay them."

"Let's make them some clothes and shoes. They must be cold in those rags," said the shoemaker.

That night, the elves were thrilled with their gifts from the shoemaker and his wife.

"Look at our new clothes!" they cried happily. And they sang:

"*Now we are so smartly dressed,
We'll give the cobbling work a rest!*"

True to their word, the elves never came back. But their shoes had made the shop famous.

The shoemaker and his wife were very grateful and were never poor again.

The Magic Porridge Pot

Once, in a small cottage on the edge of a little village, a girl named Lotte and her mother stared at their empty bowls.

They had run out of food and were very hungry.

"Go into the forest, Lotte, and find some berries," said Mother.

But Lotte couldn't find any berries.

"Don't cry, dear," said a kind old woman. "Take this iron pot. When you are hungry, just say 'Cook, *little pot, cook!*'"

"It will make the sweetest porridge. And if you say 'Stop, little pot, stop!' it will stop cooking."

"Thank you," Lotte said gratefully.

When Lotte got home, she did as the woman had said. To her delight the pot filled to the brim with sweet porridge.

"Stop, little pot, stop!" she said, and the pot stopped.

The porridge was so tasty that after Lotte had gone to school, her mother tried the pot again.

But she had forgotten the words to make it stop.

The little pot kept on cooking! The porridge quickly filled Lotte's cottage.

Then it spilled out of the door and onto the street.

Soon, the whole village was covered in porridge. But the pot kept cooking.

Lotte saw all the porridge. She ran out of the school and cried, "Stop, little pot, stop!"

Lotte had saved the village, and now everyone had plenty to eat. Everyone who liked porridge, at least!